This book
belongs to

....

....

This book is lovingly dedicated to those who inspired my love for Mathematics.

With heartfelt gratitude, I especially honour my mum Asha, my grandparents, Uncle Robin, Aunty Tara, Aunty Dhammu, Aunty Jolly, and Aunty Sally.

Love,
Jules

Millie's Meaningless Maths Mission

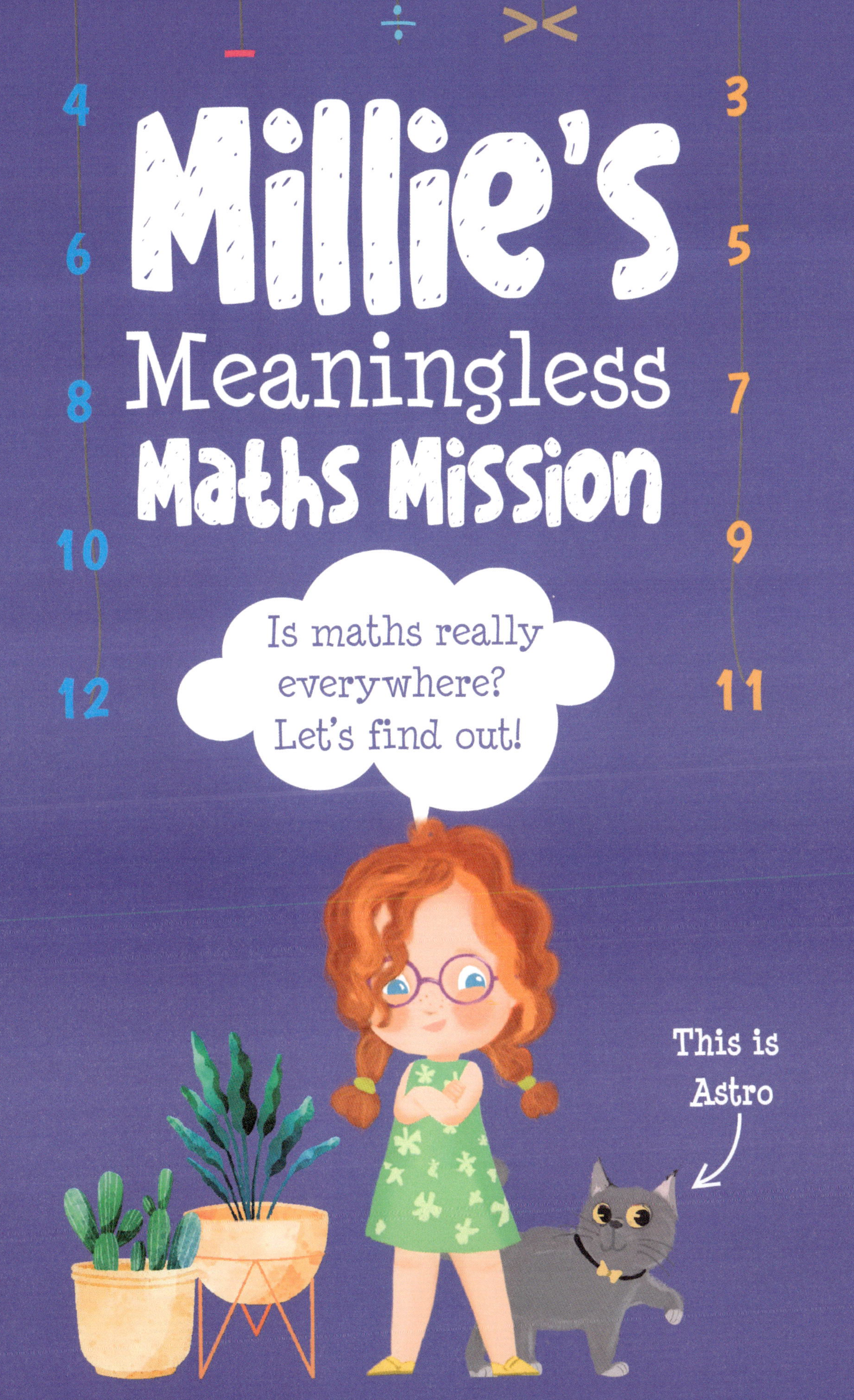

Millie stared at the numbers, shapes and squiggles in front of her. She thought sums were sooooo boring!

Her scientist dad enquired, "Why the long face?"

Millie groaned, "Maths is meaningless! And I'm not doing my homework!"

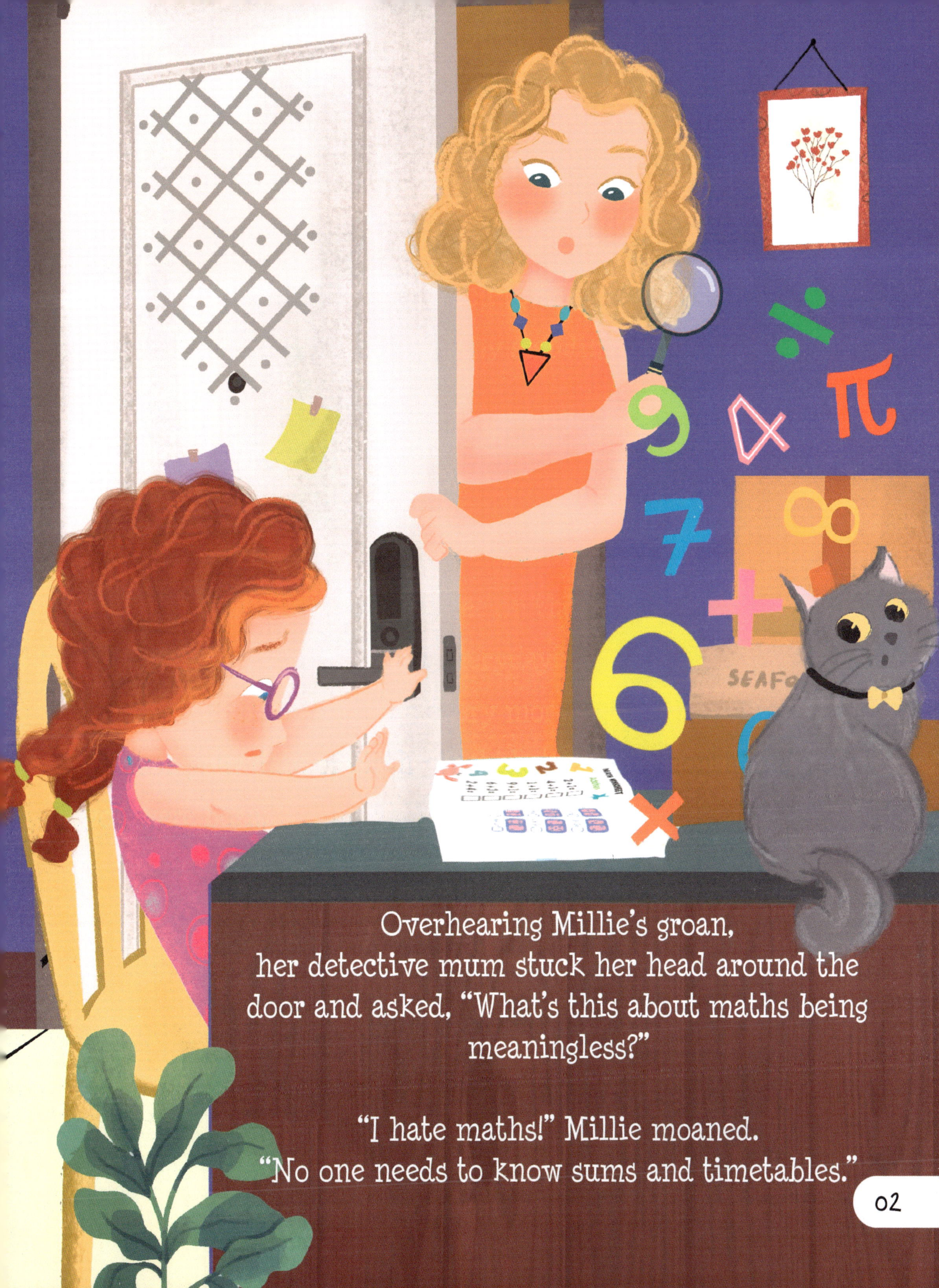

Overhearing Millie's groan, her detective mum stuck her head around the door and asked, "What's this about maths being meaningless?"

"I hate maths!" Millie moaned. "No one needs to know sums and timetables."

Her mum raised an eyebrow.
"Darling, that doesn't sound right."

Her dad twitched his nose.
"I wouldn't be
so sure about that."

"Nah ah!" said Millie.
"Teachers invented maths to bore children. No one actually uses it!"

Chuckling, her dad said, "How about a challenge? If you can go a whole day without using maths, then you don't have to do your homework."

Then her mum added,
"THAT'S A GREAT IDEA! Prove that maths
is useless and you can give it up forever!"
No more maths **ever again**!
"Hurray!" shouted Millie.
"Come on Astro,
let's goooooo!"
Oh yes!
I love a mission!

Millie was certain that proving how pointless maths was would be as easy as pie.

She spotted her friend Jasmine kicking a football in the park. She ran over and told her all about her **maths is meaningless mission.**

Jasmine was **counting** her keepie-uppies, as she declared, "Everyone knows maths is awful!"

I know, Maths is very awful," said Millie, as she kicked the ball that Jasmine passed her.

She misjudged her aim and the ball **zoomed** through the air ,whizzed over the fence and disappeared into a neighbours back garden.

"Oops!", said Millie.
Aiming to find the right house, Millie swiftly **counted, "Five, six, seven, eight...**

"It's this one!", said Millie, as she knocked on the door.

A man wearing a shirt covered in colourful **shapes** flung it open and cheerfully sang.

"Good morning little neighbours! How can I help you?"

"Hello Mr.Charles, we accidentally kicked the ball into your back garden", said Jasmine.

Mr.Charles thinks for a moment. "I'm afraid there's no ball this way, have a nice day.", he warbled.

"Oops! I think you **miscounted** the gardens Millie", said Jasmine. "It was the **seventh** house along, not the **eighth!**" they chuckled.

Jasmine finally got her ball back and Millie left to continue with her **maths is meaningless mission.**

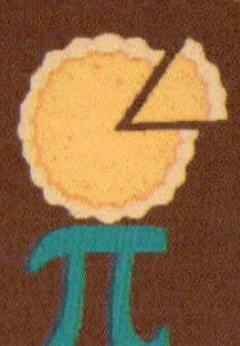

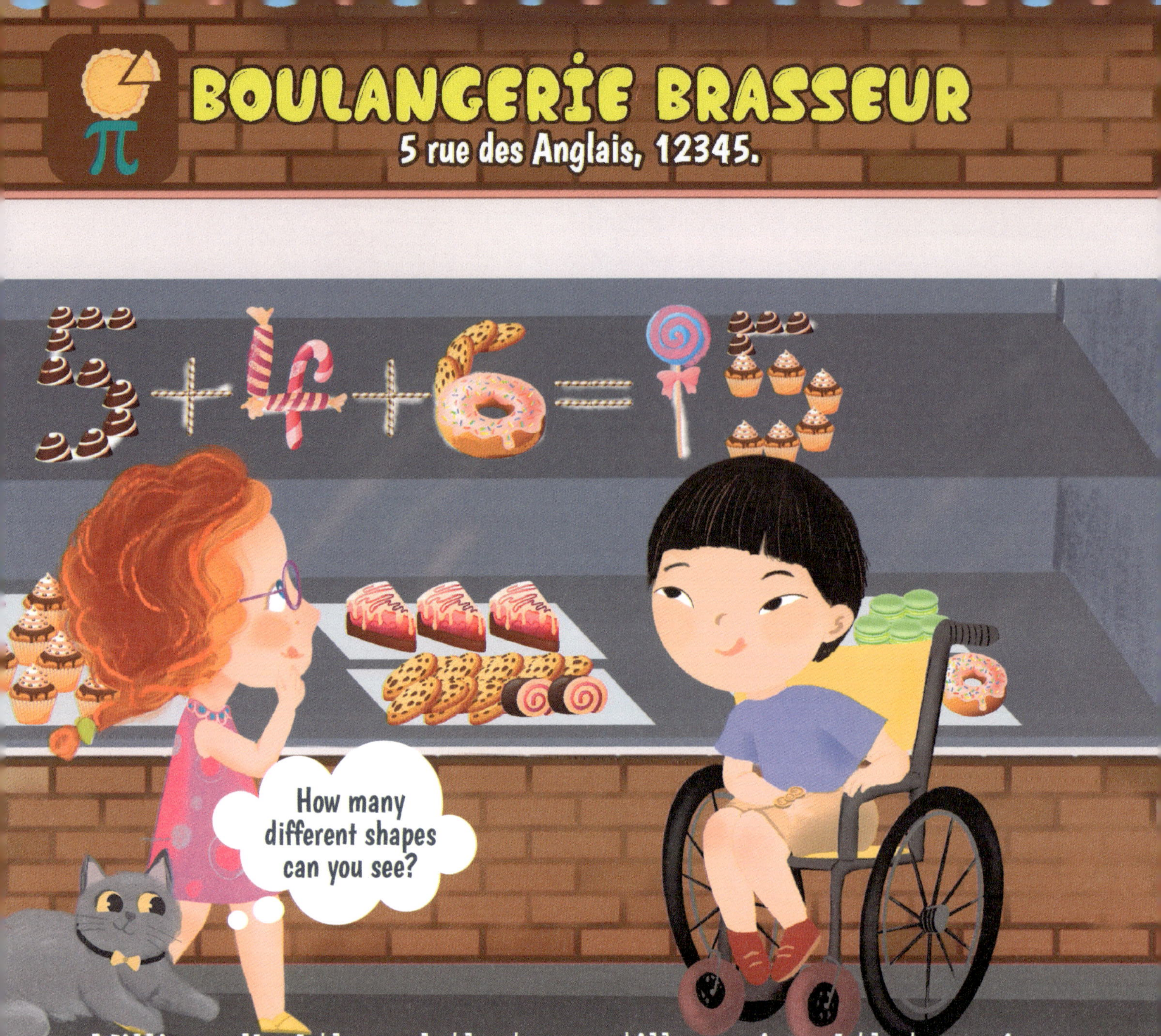
BOULANGERIE BRASSEUR
5 rue des Anglais, 12345.
5+4+6=15
How many different shapes can you see?

Millie walked through the town, still convinced that proving that maths was pointless would be a piece of cake.

She spotted her friend Haruto outside of the bakery. She hopped over and told him all about her

maths is meaningless mission.

As Haruto **counted** the change in his hand, he claimed, “Everyone knows maths is terrible!”

"I know, maths is very terrible!" exclaimed Millie, as she stared at the doughnuts in the bakery.
"I want a chocolate one. No... custard... mmm"
The baker smiled at them and said, "Can I interest you in our baker's dozen offer?"
Millie was certain that this meant **two**, and she nodded her head in agreement.
This is Mr. Luca.
The Best Baker in town.
special offer
buy a dozen of
just for
£6.50

...But the baker kept on shovelling more and more doughnuts into a **big** box and then passed it to them. It wasn't two at all...

Millie suddenly remembered her gran once telling her that a dozen was **twelve** but a baker's dozen was **thirteen!**

In the olden days, bakers got in trouble if they accidentally missed a roll out of a dozen. So, they added an extra one to prevent being told off.

Both Millie and Haruto had to **add** up and use all of their pocket money to pay for the doughnuts.

Feeling full, Millie went for a walk.

She was still certain that proving that maths was pointless would be easy peasy.

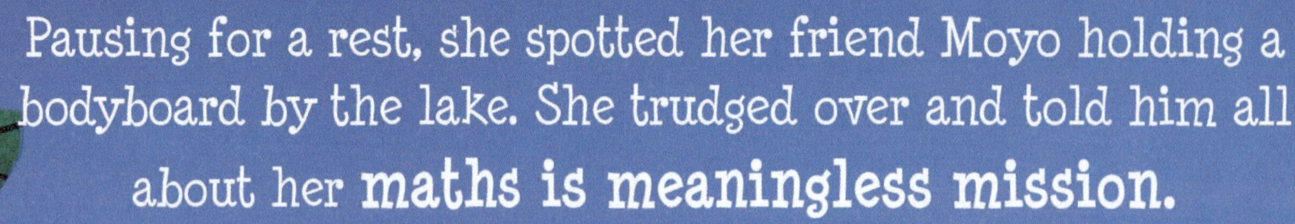

Pausing for a rest, she spotted her friend Moyo holding a bodyboard by the lake. She trudged over and told him all about her **maths is meaningless mission.**

As Moyo wiggled his toes in the water, he insisted, “Everyone knows maths is horrible!”

"I know. Maths is very horrible!" Millie exclaimed as she joined Moyo on the bodyboard.

Both children flapped their hands in the water and propelled themselves forward.

Then Millie saw a big, scaly, shiny fish lurking beneath the water. She screamed and started waving her arms around.

Then she started to move towards Moyo's side of the board. Moyo noticed the board begin to tip and yelled, "You're **unbalancing** us! Stay on your side."

But Millie didn't listen and continued to crawl forwards, which meant the board was too heavy on one side, **flipping it over!**

A rather soggy Millie was still convinced that proving maths was pointless would be a breeze. She spotted her younger cousin Stacey by the duck pond.

She squelched over to her and told her all about her **maths is meaningless mission.** As Stacey held out a packet of duck food, she said, "Everyone knows maths is silly!"

"I know. Maths is very silly!" Millie exclaimed, as she tried to keep track of the ducks Stacey hadn't fed yet. She **counted** and **recounted** them and got very confused!

Suddenly a brown duck started chasing Millie. QUACK! QUACK! QUACK!

Millie realised that due to her **miscounting**, the brown duck did not get any food!

She ran all the way home, then kicked off her soggy, squelchy, squeaky trainers.

Grinning and taking her homework book to the bin, she said, "Ha, I win! I didn't use maths. Not **once**!

Feeling victorious, Millie was about to throw her maths homework in the bin.

Her dad said, "Are you sure about that?"

"Yes, **positive, 100%** sure!" she nodded. I told you maths was meaningless.

Her mum smiled, looked at the clock and then said, "Hmm, it's 4 o'clock and time for some tea. Why don't you tell us all about your day?"

"Well, I met Jasmine at the park and accidentally kicked her ball into a garden.

But I **miscounted** the front doors and knocked on the wrong one. This funny singing man with **shapes** on his shirt answered.

Then I met Haruto at the bakery. I got confused with what a baker's **dozen** was and ordered it by mistake.

We used all of our pocket money to pay for them. Then Haruto ate **three** doughnuts in a row and said I could have the rest as he felt sick."

"Then I met Moyo at the lake and went on his bodyboard. Only I saw this scary fish and **unbalanced** us and we fell in.

Balancing

Then I met Stacey by the duck pond. I helped her count the ducks so she didn't feed them **twice** but I made a mistake and a hungry duck chased me."

Then her chuckling mum added, "Millie, it sounds like you used maths a lot. If you'd used it correctly you wouldn't have gone to the wrong door, bought too many doughnuts, fallen in the lake, or been chased by a duck."

Millie thinks about this and suddenly realises that her mum's right. Her day was packed full of **counting, numbers, and sums.**

WAIT!

Maths is actually **NOT** *meaningless*, **awful**, terrible, horrible or *silly* after all. Instead, maths really is...

EVERYWHERE!

Jasmine
Haruto
Stacey
Can you count the letters in the children's names?

The next day, at the school band practice, Millie was talking about maths with her friends when their substitute music teacher walked in.

Hmmm. He looked rather familiar! It was Mr.Charles!

"Children, feel the music," he sang, as he waved his arms about. "Bring the notes to life, on **3, 2, 1!**"

Millie strummed her guitar in **time** to the **tempo.** Jasmine blew her clarinet at the correct moment. Haruto played his piano perfectly.

But Moyo, who was on the drums, misjudged his timings and...

THUD! CRASH!

BANG! WALLOP!

"Wow! Maths is even in music," Millie shouted over the din. "We use it to read music, to know when to start playing our instruments and how long to hold our notes for."

"Oh! You're right," Moyo nodded.

"When it's used wrongly then things get noisy!" Millie grinned.

Maths is musical. Maths is fun!

Maths is everywhere!

Let's explore Maths in your everyday life.

Shapes:

- How many shapes can you find in this book?
- How many shapes can you see in your house?
- How many shapes can you draw on a piece of paper using things in your home?
- How many different shapes can you make with your fingers?

Counting:

- Count and add all the letters in the children's names in this book.
- Can you count all the books in your bedroom?
- How many fruits do you have in your house?
- How many one legged hops can you do in a row?

Adding:

- Add all your toes, fingers, elbows and knees together.
- How many cups of water did you drink today?
- Can you add up how much pocket money you have?
- Add all the legs in your house. Don't forget tables, chairs etc.

Measuring:

- How many steps does it take you to walk from home to school?
- How tall are you? No cheating by standing on your tiptoes!
- How much do you weigh?
- What size shoes do you wear?

Time:

- How many numbers can you see on the clock?
- What time do you go to bed everyday?
- What time do you wake up every morning?
- What is your date of birth - include the date, month and year you were born.

A heartfelt thank you to my family for your unwavering support and encouragement, and to my friends for your invaluable feedback.

Special thanks to my wonderful students at the Maths Club; your enthusiasm and curiosity inspired every page of this book.

Alex & Wathmi, thank you for being so patient and helping me shape this book that will hopefully help many young minds.

This journey would not have been possible without all of you.

Sincerely,
Jules